www.raintreepublishers.co.uk
Visit our website to find out
more information about
Raintree books.

To order:
☎ Phone 0845 6044371
🖹 Fax +44 (0) 1865 312263
🖳 Email myorders@raintreepublishers.co.uk

Customers from outside the UK please telephone +44 1865 312262

Raintree is an imprint of Capstone Global Library
Limited, a company incorporated in England and
Wales having its registered office at 7 Pilgrim Street,
London, EC4V 6LB - Registered company number:
6695582

Text © Capstone Global Library Limited 2010
First published in hardback in 2010
Paperback edition first published in 2011
The moral rights of the proprietor have
been asserted.

Edited by Rebecca Vickers
Designed by Steven Mead
Picture research by Ruth Blair
Production by Victoria Fitzgerald
Originated by Capstone Global Library Ltd
Printed and bound in China by South China
Printing Company Ltd

ISBN 978 0 431 11615 0 (hardback)
14 13 12 11 10
10 9 8 7 6 5 4 3 2 1
ISBN 978 0 431 11622 8 (paperback)
14 13 12 11 10
10 9 8 7 6 5 4 3 2 1

British Library Cataloguing in Publication Data
Spilsbury, Louise.
   The changing role of women since 1900. --
(Research it!)
   305.4'2'072-dc22

Acknowledgements
We would like to thank the following for permission
to reproduce photographs: Alamy: pp. 51 (©
Grapheast), 49 (© INTERFOTO Pressebildagentur),
15 (© David Noton Photography), 43 (© RFStock),
13 (© Michael Ventura); © Corbis: p. 39 (Bettmann);
Getty Images: pp. 16 (Ramzi Haidar/AFP), 14, 37
(Hulton Archive), 27 (Popperfoto); Mary Evans
Picture Library: p. 31; © The National Archives: p. 33
left; © National Portrait Gallery, London: p. 33 right;
PA Photos:
p. 41 (Dennis Cook/AP); © Rex Features:
pp. 5, 11 (Design Pics Inc), 10 (Roger-Viollet);
©shutterstock and ©iStockphoto: design features
and b/g images.

The main cover image of the suffragette protest is
reproduced with permission of Corbis/Bettmann, and
the main cover image of the suffragette magazine
is reproduced with permission of Corbis/Michael
Nicholson. The background images are reproduced
with the permission of the following: iStockphoto (©
Olena Druzhynina, © Boros Emese,
© Clifford Mueller, © Bill Noll) and shutterstock
(© Sascha Burkard, © Lars Lindblad, © Al Mueller,
©Picsfive).

The publisher would like to thank the United Nations
Organization for permission to reproduce the web
page on page 23. This was downloaded on 30 March
2009.

We would like to thank Stewart Ross for his
invaluable help in the preparation of this book.

Every effort has been made to contact copyright
holders of material reproduced in this book. Any
omissions will be rectified in subsequent printings if
notice is given to the publishers.

Contents

Researching Women's History...........................4

How Has the Role of Women Changed?......8

Making a Start....................................18

Examining Your Sources.....................30

Using Your Research..........................42

Glossary..52

Find Out More...................................54

Index...56

Some words are printed in bold, **like this**. You can find out what they mean by looking in the glossary.

Researching Women's History

The role and status of women changed more rapidly in the **western world** during the 20th century than in any other period of history. In 1900, few women had the right to vote in elections and most were not in control of their own lives and instead were treated as secondary to their husbands, fathers, and even brothers! During the course of the 20th century, which saw two world wars and dramatic advances in transport, technology, and communications, women's role altered dramatically. By 2000 most women had gained the right to vote and many had gained a more independent life than women a century earlier would have believed possible.

However, there is still much debate about whether all the changes, or the impacts of those changes, are necessarily positive, and there is still a long way to go to win equal rights for all the world's women. Around the globe women's roles are still changing, making this a hugely relevant and exciting history topic to research and study.

Why research?

People research because they want to find out things for themselves. You may choose a topic like this to research out of your own interest, or because you need to find information to write an essay or report, help you answer exam questions, or make an oral presentation. Researching women's history is challenging. Until the early 1970s, women's history was not really a subject that was studied. Topics such as women's **suffrage** (right to vote) were only just mentioned in most history textbooks. This book provides some of the facts, but to fill in gaps in your knowledge you will need to carry out your own research.

We can research and find out about the past from the wealth of information available in books, on the Internet, and from many other sources. This can be a bit like looking for a needle in a haystack, so this book will look at the techniques and approaches you will need to research and answer questions about the changing role of women since 1900. As well as helping you find information, it will also explain some of the research skills you will need to sort, evaluate, and understand that information.

Research challenges

Your research challenge may be to answer a variety of questions on women's changing role and status in the 20th century. Here are a few examples:

- Why were some women in the UK given the vote in parliamentary elections in 1918?
- How significant was the impact of the two world wars on the role and status of women?
- How did opportunities for women change from 1900 to 2000?

Don't think of research as a dry, boring thing to do. One way to bring history research alive is to get first-hand accounts of the past, perhaps from older relatives or friends. Ask women what their and their mothers' lives were like in the past. What changes have they experienced in their lifetimes, and what is their opinion of those changes?

Understanding information

One reason you can now find an enormous amount of research information on the topic of women's changing role in history is because it is a topic about which people have strong views. This means that sometimes the books or other sources that you read will contain attitudes and opinions as well as facts.

For example, a historian may focus only on the way women were **oppressed** and not mention the positive aspects of their lives at a particular time or in a particular place. This may represent a **biased** view. That is why it is vital to use more than one source to find out about a person or event in the past when researching a history topic like this one. To be able to get a full picture of the past you will need to understand and extract information from different kinds of sources and cross-check and confirm dates and other kinds of information.

The research process

You can think of the research process as eight simple steps, which we will look at in more depth throughout the book. If you follow these steps, you cannot go far wrong:

Step 1 Gain an overview. Get an idea of the topic in a wider context.

Step 2 Decide what you need to know. Link your research to your question or study topic.

Step 3 Research information using many sources, including books and the Internet.

Step 4 Look at images and learn how to "read" them, and how to use them.

Step 5 Make thorough and well referenced research notes.

Step 6 Evaluate your research.

Step 7 Organize your research notes.

Step 8 Present your findings.

A variety of sources

Research gives you a chance to use a variety of sources of information. Generally there are two kinds of source: primary and secondary. **Primary sources** are original, first-hand accounts of events, such as official documents like prison records or wills created at the time the historical events occurred,

artefacts (objects that existed at the time), and sources such as letters, diaries, and newspaper reports written by people at the time of an event or not long after it happened.

Secondary sources are those created after an event and have usually been created using different primary sources. They often mention primary sources or use **quotes** from them. Secondary sources include history textbooks and biographies of famous people. Because secondary sources are often published books they are usually easier to find than primary sources. Ideally, you will use a wide mix of primary and secondary sources in your research.

Types of source

PRIMARY	SECONDARY
Diaries/memoirs	History textbooks
Letters	Biographies
Photographs	Journal articles
News film	Academic works
Sound recordings	Encyclopedias
Newspaper stories	TV documentaries
Eyewitness accounts	Films
Military reports	
Government reports	

When were they made?

At the time of an event, or very soon after	Created after event; sometimes a long time after something happened

Who created them?

Someone who saw or heard an event themselves; they may express an opinion or argument about a past event	Someone who wasn't there often using a range of primary or other secondary sources; it may express an opinion or argument about a past event

How common are they?

Often one-of-a-kind, or rare	More commonly available

How Has the Role of Women Changed?

The history of women's **rights** or role and status in society is a challenging topic to research because it can be looked at from so many different angles – by country, by time period, by themes such as politics or education, or by famous or important personalities. That is why a good place to start your research is with general reference sources, such as an encyclopedia or general history books (in print or online). These will help you to get an overview of the general topic or a particular period. If you don't know a great deal about your subject, an overview provides you with a basic understanding of it and a platform from which to extend your research. This will help you think about what else you need to look for online or in print at the next stage. When doing your own research you will come across some of the themes and topics that follow.

From the 1900s

Your starting point for research could be that in 1900 most women across the world had few rights. Few had the right to vote in general elections and in many countries the woman's realm was the home. Women were responsible for looking after children and household work, such as cleaning and cooking, in their own homes or for other people. Most middle-class women left home only when they married, and then everything they owned was transferred from their fathers to their husbands. Divorce was not an option for most women, however unhappy or abusive their marriages were.

In 1900 there was no welfare system and also no free healthcare. Many women were weakened by frequent pregnancies, and large numbers died in childbirth, because they did not have proper medical care.

Many women did not have access to education, and those who did usually did not get the same educational opportunities as boys. For others, education was considered a waste of time as they were destined to be wives and mothers. Although a few rich women trained and worked as doctors or in other professions, throughout the world most women worked in the fields, as servants, or in manual jobs, for long hours and for low or no wages.

The birth of women's rights

Before 1900, there had already been many calls for change. During the French Revolution, a writer and political activist, Olympe de Gouge, published her *Declaration of the Rights of Woman and the Female Citizen* (1791). In Britain in 1792 Mary Wollstonecraft wrote *A Vindication of the Rights of Woman*, a book that argued for educational and social rights for women. In 1848 in the USA, women's rights activist Elizabeth Cady Stanton presented the *Declaration of Rights and Sentiments* at a historic meeting. This document demanded that women be allowed to take an equal part in society alongside men, including the right to vote in elections. Stanton and another campaigner, Susan B. Anthony, founded the U.S. National Women Suffrage Association in 1869. In Australia, Vida Goldstein actively promoted women's rights and founded the National Council of Women in 1888.

Individual women had also made progress through changing laws. For example, in the UK Caroline Norton campaigned for the 1857 Matrimonial Causes Act that allowed divorce through the law courts and reformed laws controlling property rights for married women and the custody of children. In 1849, Elizabeth Blackwell became the first woman to earn a medical degree in the United States. Political campaigner, Elizabeth Garrett Anderson, became the first English woman to qualify as a doctor in 1865. Her success inspired the act of 1876 that permitted women to enter the medical professions.

Female sphere   **Male sphere**

housework, childcare, caring for the sick, running the home, cleaning and cooking

attending church, charitable works, self-improvement

making laws, fighting in wars, running businesses, controlling property and finances

Venn diagrams like this one are useful for contrasting and comparing information. This one shows the differences in the upper middle class between the private female sphere of influence and responsibility and the public male sphere that still dominated in 1900. The area in the middle shows areas where both women and men had similar responsibilities.

Suffragettes and suffragists

An important theme in the study of women's changing role during the early years of the 20th century is the struggle for women's suffrage – the right to vote. This would allow women to influence governments who made decisions about their lives. Women who campaigned for suffrage were called **suffragists** or **suffragettes**. The suffragists had more members and held meetings and peaceful processions.

The suffragettes had fewer members, but are more renowned because they carried out more extreme protests. In the UK, a minority of British suffragettes chained themselves to railings, broke windows, and ended up in prison. The *Daily Mail* newspaper in January 1906 dubbed these women "suffragettes" as a term of abuse, but many women in the UK and USA defiantly adopted the term. The movement for women's suffrage developed around the world, in women's associations in China, India, and Egypt, for example, and in many places with the support of men.

Throughout Western Europe women were campaigning for the vote. This demonstration was held in Paris in 1914.

The impact of World War I

With the outbreak of World War I in 1914 the struggle for suffrage was put on hold because most suffragettes (and suffragists) joined the war effort, for example, by helping to recruit young men to the army. In spite of the reduction in direct campaigning for suffrage at this time, many people believe that the changes in women's role during the war helped them to achieve the vote after the war was over. When men left to fight in the war, industries in their home countries required workers and women stepped in.

Women worked in many industries they would never have been able to before, from weapons factories, to public transport, to government offices, to ship building.

After the war, these same women lost their jobs to make way for the men coming back home, but attitudes towards women and their rights had shifted and around the world women gained the vote. In countries such as the Soviet Union and countries in Eastern Europe, Communist revolutions brought hardships, but they granted women equal rights, too, often long before women in the West won such rights. In 1918 the Soviet Union introduced **maternity leave**, government-funded child care, equal pay for equal work, equal education, and the right to hold any political office.

During World War I women filled many positions brought into existence by wartime needs. Women were welcomed into jobs and industries that had previously excluded them. In some countries this changed immediately after the war was over. For example, in the UK the Pre-War Practices Act of 1919 excluded women from many skilled jobs, and the "marriage bar" forced women to resign from many jobs once they were married.

Women's suffrage victories

Here are some dates from around the world when women gained the right to vote in at least some elections:

1893	New Zealand		
1902	Australia (except Aboriginal peoples)	1934	Brazil
		1944	Jamaica, France
1906	Finland	1945	Italy, Japan
1915	Denmark	1949	China, India
1917	Soviet Union, Canada	1952	Mexico
1918	Germany, The Netherlands, Britain (women aged 30 and over)	1956	Egypt
		1964	Kenya
		1971	Switzerland
1920	USA	1974	Jordan
1932	Ceylon (now Sri Lanka)		

Between the wars

In spite of initial setbacks after the end of World War I in terms of work, the 1920s brought new freedoms and changes for many women and advances in women's education. More universities opened to women, and more women gained college degrees than ever before. In 1928, U.S. women earned 39 percent of college degrees compared to 19 percent in 1900.

The issue of women's access to **contraception** also came to the fore when Margaret Sanger set up the first **birth-control** clinic in the USA in 1916, and Marie Stopes opened a birth-control clinic in London in 1921. Although few women had access to these clinics, it was the beginning of a major change that would allow women more freedom to pursue their own careers and goals. Another change was in the world of sport. In 1900 women were expected to do "ladylike" sports, such as dancing and horse-riding. In the 1928 Olympics, women were finally allowed to compete in gymnastics and athletics events.

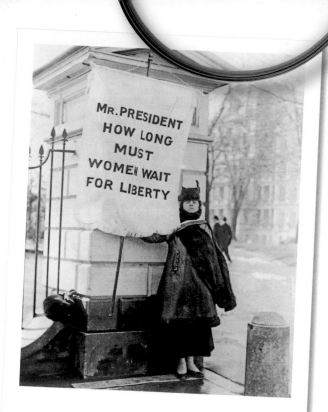

American suffragettes and campaigners for women's rights often picketed the White House and other government buildings in Washington, D.C.

World War II

During World War II (1939–1945) women played an even more active role than they had done in World War I. As well as taking on men's work in their home countries, many women joined the armed services, for example, as pilots in the UK, USA, and Soviet Union. To make it easier for women to work, nurseries were set up in the UK to look after children while their mothers were out, and part-time work was introduced in several countries so that women could fit work in with their other responsibilities at home. However, women were still paid less than men for doing the same work.

Defining "women's work"

After World War II, some governments expected women to return home and leave the jobs free for men who were returning from war. In some countries, such as France, women came under pressure from politicians to stay at home to have more children to help rebuild the economy after the war. More babies meant more demand for goods and services and more workers and consumers for the future. In France, the government introduced a series of allowances that were given to women according to how many children they had. This was not the case in countries such as the Soviet Union where women continued to work in many areas, such as engineering and labouring, deemed "men's work" in the West. Today, the definition of what jobs are suitable for women is still hotly debated. For example, in some armies, women fight on the front line alongside men in war situations, but some officers and civilians argue that women are not physically or emotionally suited to the front line and should leave this "work" to men.

The 1960s and 1970s

In 1963 a landmark book called *The Feminine Mystique* by American feminist Betty Friedan was published. Dedicated to French feminist and philosopher Simone de Beauvoir, who first used the term "women's liberation", Friedan called for women to look beyond the role of homemaker. She wasn't alone. In the West during the 1960s and 1970s, the "women's liberation" political movement campaigned on a number of issues, such as equal pay and equal rights at work. Among the most active groups was the National Organization of Women (NOW) formed in 1966 in the USA.

Many more women joined the workforce during this period. For example, in the USA the number increased to 43 percent in 1969, compared to 25 percent in 1940, although women's wages were only still only 60 percent of men's. Also, in the 1960s laws were passed that made it easier for couples to get divorced. The 1960s saw more women taking important government roles. In 1960, Sirimavo Bandaranaike became the first democratically elected female national leader when she became prime minister in Sri Lanka, followed by Indira Gandhi in India in 1966, and Golda Meir in Israel in 1969.

Sirimavo Bandaranaike ran for office in Sri Lanka in 1960 after her husband, who had been prime minister, was assassinated. Here she is shown campaigning on behalf of the Freedom Party.

Politics and education today

Today, most women around the world have the vote and many take important roles in government and politics. In Rwanda, women make up about half the government. However, women still do not have the vote in a handful of countries, including Saudi Arabia, and worldwide women hold only 14 percent of parliamentary seats. In terms of education, a much higher percentage of girls and women today go to school and college than in 1900. However, 800 million people worldwide are still **illiterate** and almost two-thirds of these are women. An interesting avenue for research might be to compare and contrast the status of women in different countries with your own, or others. For example, did you know that in Iran more than 65 percent of university students are women, or that in Africa more than 40 percent of women do not have access to even the most basic education?

A woman's right to choose?

In the 1960s, NOW and many other feminist groups fought for legal **abortions**, which they said was about a woman's right to choose whether or not to have a child. By the 1970s women had been granted restricted rights to abortion in the West, but this remains a hotly debated issue the world over, as those against abortion say they are defending the rights of the unborn child. Many people argue that a more important issue is that many women do not have adequate medical care, especially during pregnancy. Globally, over half a million women die in pregnancy and childbirth every year and 99 percent of these deaths occur in developing countries. The contraceptive pill, available from the 1960s, gave women the ability to choose when and whether to have children. One research line to follow could be to find out about the influence and profile of prominent campaigners on women's right to choose, such as Gloria Steinem (who also co-founded the feminist magazine Ms in 1972).

Women's status today

Some women – including Helen Greiner, co-founder and board member of iRobot, the largest robot company in the world – do succeed in business. However, globally women are still paid less than men in general and still hold only a small proportion of the senior jobs in influential careers such as business, politics, and the law. And it is not simply the case that women fare better in the West: in 2008 fewer than 20 percent of MPs in the UK were women, compared to 27.7 percent in Afghanistan, and 25.5 percent in Iraq. The difficulties some women have combining motherhood and work today, such as childcare problems, the sharing of domestic chores, and discrimination against working mothers, would make an interesting research topic.

According to the UN, women work two-thirds of the world's working hours, and produce half of the world's food. Yet they earn only ten percent of the world's income, and own less than one percent of the world's property.

Timeline

This timeline shows a selection of significant dates in the history of women's changing role in the 20th century:

Date	Event
1900	Suffragists start to campaign in many parts of the world
1902	Women in Australia get the vote
1912	Sylvia Pankhurst establishes London Federation of Suffragettes
1918	Women over 30 in UK get the right to vote
1920	Women 21 and over in the USA get the right to vote; Oxford University opens its degrees to women
1922	The UK Law of Property Act enables wives to inherit property equally
1928	Women compete for the first time in Olympic field events
1932	Amelia Earhart is the first woman to fly the Atlantic Ocean solo
1937	American Medical Association (AMA) drops its official opposition to birth control
1941	Women in the UK conscripted (made to do) to perform war work
1944	Women in France get the right to vote
1953	*The Second Sex* by French feminist writer Simone De Beauvoir published in the USA (first published in France in 1949); contains first use of phrase "women's liberation"
1960	Sirimavo Bandaranaike of Sri Lanka is the first democratically elected female national leader
1961	The contraceptive pill goes on sale for the first time in the UK
1963	Russian Lt. Col Valentina Tereshkova is the first woman in space
1966	National Organization for Women (NOW) founded in the USA
1966	Indira Gandhi becomes the first female prime minister of India
1967	Abortion Law makes some abortions legal in Britain
1969	Golda Meir becomes the first female prime minister of Israel
1970	Equal Pay Act (UK) makes legal equal pay for women
1971	The USA passes a law banning sex discrimination in employment
1972	Launch of feminist magazine *Ms*, co-founded by Gloria Steinem
1974	The U.S. Coalition of Labor Union Women (CLUW) founded by women labour union leaders, with the aim of increasing women's involvement in their unions
1975	The Sex Discrimination Act in the UK makes it illegal to discriminate against women in education, recruitment, and advertising
1975	The United Nations' Decade for Women begins, during which time the UN runs several conferences to examine women's living conditions around the world
1979	Margaret Thatcher elected the first UK female prime minister
1988	Benazir Bhutto becomes the first female prime minister of Pakistan
1993	First "Take Our Daughters to Work Day" in the USA
1997	The England women's cricket team first competes wearing trousers
1997	Madeleine Albright is the first female Secretary of State in the USA
2003	Iranian lawyer and human rights activist Shirin Ebadi awarded Nobel Peace Prize for her efforts for the rights of women and children
2005	Angela Merkel becomes Germany's first woman chancellor

Challenges facing women's status

Women's status is still at issue in many places, for example, in countries where tradition and/or religious beliefs can be a barrier to equal rights. Here are a few examples:

- Under the Muslim law of inheritance, a daughter is eligible for only half the share of property given to a son.
- In Pakistan, men are entitled to take the law into their own hands for the sake of the family's "honour" and murder wives, daughters, or sisters they suspect of adultery.
- In Afghanistan, women are murdered for working or campaigning on women's rights issues.
- In parts of some countries where families favour boy children, including India and China, many female babies are killed at birth because they are considered of low worth.

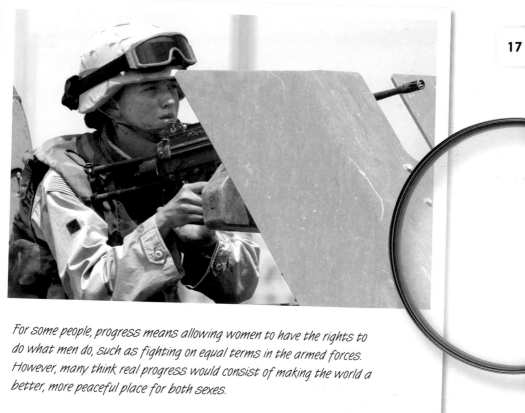

For some people, progress means allowing women to have the rights to do what men do, such as fighting on equal terms in the armed forces. However, many think real progress would consist of making the world a better, more peaceful place for both sexes.

Making a Start

When you research a topic, you need to start out by collecting background evidence and information, such as specific dates and events. That way you can piece together your own understanding of the subject. In this chapter we look at where you can find information and how to research in a successful, focused way.

The long and short of it

First, take a moment to reread the question or brief that you have been given. Check the terms of the question or title. To find out how much information you will need to research, check if it requires a short, medium, or long answer. Use a highlighter pen to highlight key numbers or words, such as the dates you are meant to cover or the main issue you should discuss. For example, does the brief cover just the war years or does it focus on a single issue, such as equal pay? This helps to focus your mind on the job in hand.

What do you know?

Whenever you are about to learn something new, it helps to start with what you already know. One way to do this is by doing a brainstorm. A brainstorm is when you give yourself a set time to jot down anything you know that is related to the topic. There are no right or wrong answers, and you should feel free just to write down anything and everything that comes into your head. When you review the brainstorming notes later, you may reject some ideas as irrelevant, but you should find that others help to set you off on your research journey.

KWL charts

Another way to organize what you need to find out is through a KWL chart. The K stands for "What I **K**now", the W for "What I **W**ant to Know", and the L for "What I **L**earned". The first two columns should be completed before you start your research. The third column should be completed after the research is done. The charts help you to find specific things to look for and when you fill in the final column, after your research is finished, it helps you to reflect on what you have learned.

What I **K**now	What I **W**ant to know	What I **L**earned
Suffragettes fought for women's rights. The women of the Pankhurst family were famous suffragettes. Some suffragettes protested by chaining themselves to railings.	Why they protested in that way? Why were they called suffragettes? Who opposed women's suffrage and why? Were the suffragettes successful?	[to be completed later]

This KWL chart was made in response to the question "Who were the suffragettes, and what did they do?"

Narrowing and broadening your topic

Sometimes in an essay or report question you may be given a very broad research topic, such as "How did women's roles change between 1900 and 2000?" This covers an overwhelming amount of information, so it is best if you break the topic down into several smaller, more manageable topics. For example, a broad topic like women's changing role could be broken down into different areas like education or equal pay or the right to vote. You could also narrow a topic down in terms of place or time. On the other hand, you may need to research a specific, narrow question such as "Who was Elizabeth Cady Stanton?" It may then help to broaden your research to understand the context of this person or event. For example, you might research the key events she was involved in and what changes she saw in her lifetime to see how she fitted into the wider history.

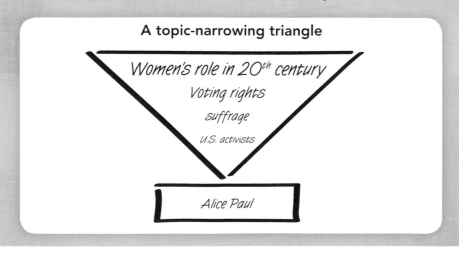

A topic-narrowing triangle

Women's role in 20th century
Voting rights
suffrage
U.S. activists

Alice Paul

Starting your research

Once you know what you want to find out, the best place to start your research is the library. Unlike many pages on the Internet (see pages 22–23), information books in a library have been checked by editors, publishers, and the librarian. Although they may not be perfect, there have been quality checks so you can trust that the information is fairly accurate. Search for reference books in your subject area, specifically those to do with women's history. Also look at general history books that cover the time period you are interested in, or search a library catalogue to find books on your topic.

Contents

Women in 1900 4
Fighting for the vote 6
Women in politics 1914–45 8
Women in politics 1945 onwards 10
Women in civil rights movements 12
Campaigning women 14
Women and human rights 16
Education of girls and women 18
Domestic life 20
Marriage, motherhood, and divorce 22
Changes since 1960 24
Healthcare and medicine 26
Women and work 1900–39 28
Women's service in World War II 30
Women's work in the postwar era 32
Women's work at the end of the century 34
Entertainment, media, and the arts 36
Fashion statements 38
Sport 40
Women's rights into the 21st century 42
Timeline 44

In this history book about women in the 20th century, a quick look down the contents list shows that you can find a reference to votes for women on page 6. Would any of the other pages be useful or of interest?

Finding your way

Once you have a history book in your hand you will want to find relevant information quickly and efficiently. An encyclopedia may be organized alphabetically or by subject, so you could flick through to "W" to see if there is a feature on "Women's rights" or "S" for "Suffragettes". Otherwise the contents list is usually your first stop. This lists the chapters or sections of a book in the order in which they appear.

Another way of finding out if a book has the information you seek without reading the whole thing is to check the **index**. You will find the index at the back of a book. It is a list of all the names, important events, and subjects covered in the book and it is laid out in alphabetical order. Pictures, graphs, and charts might be in italics, and some entries will be found under other subheadings. For example, if you are looking for laws about equal pay you may have to look under the subheading 'laws' to find specific laws on women's rights.

Sanger, Margaret 22
Seneca Falls conference 5
segregation in USA 12
sexual harassment 33
Soviet Union 9, 33
Stanton, Elizabeth Cady 5
suffrage 6, 8, 9
suffragettes and suffragists 6, 7, 24

Thatcher, Margaret 11
trade unions 28, 31, 32-33, 35

Check the index at the back of a history book to see if the book has any information about a specific person or event you are studying, for example a figure such as Elizabeth Cady Stanton or Margaret Thatcher. Don't forget that indexes list surnames first, for example Thatcher, Margaret.

Bibliographies

A **bibliography** is a list of books and other sources that an author used in writing a book. The bibliography is usually found at the end of a book. Bibliographies are useful because they may lead you to other useful books. Some bibliographies may be divided into different formats or subjects. Books in a bibliography usually give the author's name (surname first), then the book title and then other details, like the publisher and date the book was published, to help you find or order it from the library. To check whether a book is going to be a useful resource for you, look on the Internet for reviews and for more information about what it contains.

Internet research

The Internet can be a great source of information and gives you access to less well-known, and often more interesting, research topics. However, one problem with Internet research is that there is so much material out there. Finding the right information can take hours, and you will have to plough through pages and pages of irrelevant material to get to it.

Searching effectively

Access to the Internet can be done through home, school, or library computers using search engines, such as Google and Yahoo!, but if you simply type *women's changing role* into Google, for example, you will get over 12 million results! You need to search in such a way that you reduce the number of results and locate those that are most helpful.

Getting the most out of a search engine

These methods work on Google and most other search engines:

- You can force Google to exclude words by putting a minus symbol right before them. For example by using women -fashion you can search for pages about women that don't include information about fashion.
- In some search engines you can use OR to search for pages that contain either of two terms. For example, the search *women World War II OR WW II OR Second World War* allows for the fact that World War II is described in different ways.
- If you are searching for something quite specific, a good tip is to put your phrase or search words in inverted commas or double quote marks. For example, if you type in *"Gloria Steinem founded Ms"* the search engine will only list websites that include that exact phrase, rather than all of the websites that include those four words at some point.
- Focus the search by adding other relevant search words. For example, rather than just searching for *"women in politics"* you could search for *"women in politics" France*.

Quality and accuracy

The quality of information on the Internet varies a lot and you cannot trust everything you read there. There are obvious reasons for this: anyone can put a page up on the Internet – they might be a professor of women's history or an ordinary person with strong opinions on the subject. People can say anything they like and leave it there as long as they like, so you have to be careful about which information you use. For example, there are well-established online encyclopedias, such as *MSN Encarta*, *World Book* or *Encyclopaedia Britannica*, but there are also others, such as *Wikipedia*, that are written by volunteers who may or may not know what they are talking about.

Understanding a website

Start with major library and museum websites that have special learning sections and follow links from their pages, as these are likely to have been checked. Major organizations, such as the United Nations (see below), have their own websites that carry fact sheets and links. The URL is the web address of the page you are accessing. It appears at the top of your browser when you have a web page open, e.g. http://www.institute.ac.uk/. The letters after the name of the website tell you what sort of organization it is. Look for academic or educational websites that end with .ac or .edu. You might also try government sites, which end with .gov. Sites that end with .com are businesses or commercial sites and in general exist to make money, not merely to share information. Check the website for information about who wrote it, where it is from, and when it was written. Cross-check the name of the writer with other things the author has written to find out if he or she is genuinely an expert.

Skimming and scanning for information

When you have narrowed down your research techniques efficiently and found a good article on the Internet or a useful chapter in a library book you still won't have time to read every word in them. You need to develop skills in **skimming** and **scanning** so you can increase your reading speed and get the most out of a source in the minimum time.

The way to do this is to first be clear about what you are looking for. So, for example, if you are researching a paper on women's roles during the two world wars, you might be looking specifically for women in active service in World War II.

Skimming

Then you need to skim the resource to find out what information it contains about your topic. Skimming a resource means looking quickly through the headings, pictures, and first and last sentences of the different sections or paragraphs to get an idea of which parts are useful for you. In this case you might be looking for words such as "pilots", "front line", or "ATS" (Auxiliary Territorial Service), which was the women's branch of the British Army during World War II.

When you skim you should read at about twice your normal reading speed. The idea is to find paragraphs that might be useful, not to read carefully for sense at this stage.

Scanning

Scanning is a technique that helps you locate specific information, such as names, dates, or places within a piece of text. When you scan you know what you are looking for before you start reading. The idea is that you quickly scan – or glance – down the page, keeping your eye out for a key word or date.

So for example, imagine you were looking for information about the UK National Service Act of 1941, which called up unmarried women aged between 20 and 30 to work in tank and aircraft factories and for other jobs, such as driving trains and operating anti-aircraft guns. As you quickly run your eyes across and down a page you don't really read the words. Instead you look out for the date "1941" or the words "National Service Act".

The SQ3R technique

A technique called **SQ3R** can help you to examine, assess, and organize the information that you gain from your research sources. The letters SQ3R stand for **S**urvey – **Q**uestion – **R**ead – **R**ecite – **R**eview. These five steps can be very useful if you are feeling puzzled or overwhelmed by all the information you have found. To use the SQ3R technique, follow these simple steps:

Survey ...
- a work's title, chapter, and spread headings and subheadings, as well as captions to pictures, charts, graphs, and maps
- the foreword or introduction and conclusion or **summary**, looking for major ideas
- review questions and educational study guides.

Question
- Turn the title, headings, and subheadings into questions.
- Ask yourself, "What question is this section trying to answer?"
- Read any questions that appear at the end of sections or chapters.
- Ask yourself, "What did my teacher say about this subject or chapter when the project was assigned?"
- Ask yourself, "What do I already know about this subject?"

Read
- Look for answers to the questions that appear at the end of chapters or in an educational study guide.
- Reread captions to pictures, charts, graphs, and maps.
- Note all words or phrases that are underlined, italic, or bold.
- Read difficult passages more slowly.
- Stop and reread any passages that are not clear.
- Read a section at a time.

Recite
- Say questions out loud about what you have just read.
- Take notes from the text, but summarize the information in your own words.
- If using photocopies, underline or highlight important points you've just read.
- Recite answers out loud, remembering that the more sensible your answers, the more likely you are to remember what you read.

Review ...
- the key phrases and other notes you made within 24 hours of making the notes
- again after one week
- about once a month until the time of your presentation (or exam).

Timelines

What do you do with all those dates you discover in the course of your research? Producing a timeline can be an invaluable way to organize the dates and get your head round a new topic. Timelines help you order and visualize a sequence of events. Putting events on a timeline gives you a sense of how much time goes by in between each event. You can often find ready-made timelines, and it is a quick, visual way to see events in **chronological** order. However, it is much more useful to make one of your own, picking the dates relevant to your research. By doing it yourself you build up a better overview of the period.

Timeline tips

When doing a timeline for a topic, such as women's changing role, you might like to add a second layer of dates, perhaps above the timeline bar. This could contain dates of major world or national events. This helps you to see at a glance how dates are connected and sets the history of women's rights in a wider context. If you do a timeline that includes important world dates, this can be a real help when answering questions like "How did national and world events affect the role of women?"

How to make a timeline

1. The first thing to do is decide what your timeline will show. The bigger your topic or longer the period of time it covers, the more information there will be. It is best to have a focused plan to cover one topic in your timeline, like "women and health" or "women in politics".
2. Next you need to decide how you will choose events to include and exclude. Will you cover dates for the world or for just one country? Will you include general events or only those directly related to your topic?
3. Research and note the dates when the events that you wish to include occurred and write down where you found them. That way you can go back and check if the sources were reliable. Don't just accept the date given by one source. Check the date against other sources too to make sure you don't make any mistakes.
4. When you have all your dates, work out which are the earliest and latest dates that you want to include. These will set the time span.
5. Work out what size segments your timeline will be divided into. For shorter time spans you could do yearly segments. For longer periods you could do ten-year segments.
6. Put the dates on your timeline in chronological order.

Women in sport

1900 Women compete in the Paris Olympics in golf, tennis, and croquet.

1926 Gertrude Ederle is the first woman to swim the English Channel.

1948 Alice Coachman is first black woman to win Olympic gold (in the high jump).

1973 Billie Jean King defeats male opponent Bobby Riggs in the "Battle of the Sexes" tennis match.

2007 The Wimbledon tennis tournament announces it will start paying equal prize money for women and men.

1900   1915   1930   1945   1960   1975   1990   2005

1924 Only figure skating is open to women at the first Winter Olympic Games.

1928 Women compete in Olympic track and field events.

1952 Women and men compete together in Olympic equestrian events.

1984 First ever women's Olympic marathon.

2008 Danica Patrick is first woman to win a major international motor racing event when she comes first in an IndyCar race.

This is an example of a timeline about a specific topic: women in sport.

This picture of some of the women who competed in the 1928 Olympics could be used to illustrate a timeline like the one above.

Record your sources

It is important to keep a note of all the resources you use. When you find a useful source, be sure to write down details, such as the author, title, place, and date of publication. You'll need this information to **cite** the book later and so that you can check to see if the resource was accurate or to refer to it in an essay. It is a good idea to keep a record of useful sources on note cards (see above). That way you can add a brief description of what the book or article is about, too.

Ross, Mandy. 20th Century Perspectives: The Changing Role of Women. Oxford: Heinemann Library, 2002.

This book contains information on a wide range of topics. There is one spread on changes since the 1960s on pages 24-25.

Note taking

When you find a useful resource, you might be able to photocopy the page (so long as you mark on it where the information came from), but usually you will take notes about it on cards or sheets. You can do this in several ways:

- Write a summary sentence that sums up what you have learned.
- Use paraphrasing. **Paraphrases** are your own version of information that you have read, and then rewritten in your own words.
- Copy useful sentences of text to use as **quotes**, so long as you credit the people who said or wrote them.
- Write notes for different topics on different coloured cards, or using clear headings on sheets of notes, so that you can see at a glance what topic they cover.

Data capture sheets

One way to combine notes, dates, and lists of sources is in a data capture sheet on a computer. This is when data is stored in a table with rows and columns beneath column headings. Many tables and reports can be stored in the same database file. The table on page 29 is about the attempts to get an Equal Rights Amendment (ERA) in the USA (a law to guarantee equal treatment of men and women in all areas of life) since the 1960s. The U.S. Constitution still remains without an ERA because several states refused to accept it. You could add extra columns, for example, one for notes on the reliability of the sources.

Source	What does this source show?	How can I use this source?	Where is this source from?
Graph comparing male and female earnings 1960–2000	In 1960 women earned at least a third less than men	As evidence that women earned less than men and suggests they also had lower status jobs	U.S. Government Census Bureau records (found on website www.census.gov/prod/2004pubs/p60-226.pdf)
Statement of Purpose from National Women's Organization (NOW) at their first conference in 1966	It shows the aims of the male and female members of NOW	It shows that men and women were still fighting for equal pay and opportunities in 1966	At NOW's website www.now.org/history/purpos66.html
Encyclopedia explanation of the Equal Rights Amendment (ERA) 1972	It shows that the ERA is intended to ban all laws that give one sex different rights than the other	It tells us the history of the ERA and some of the arguments for and against it.	Online encyclopedia www.worldbook.com
News magazine article from 1980 about a demonstration in Chicago of people demanding that the state of Illinois sign up for the ERA	It shows that just because the law was passed, not everyone agreed with it and some states were slow to sign up to it	It tells us that the members of NOW and other feminists still had to fight for equal rights long after 1972	*Time* magazine article, May 26 1980 (www.time.com)

Summing it up: How to research

Here are some top tips on how to successfully research your topic:
- First work out what you know and exactly what it is you want to find out.
- Use as many sources as possible, from the library to the Internet.
- Check sources are accurate and reliable, especially when using the Internet.
- Keep a full record of all your sources so you can quote from them later.
- Make careful notes in an organized way so that you can retrieve the information later.

Examining Your Sources

How you judge the resources you use in your research is vitally important. Some people make the mistake of thinking that primary sources, such as newspaper accounts, letters, or photos, are "truer" than secondary sources, such as textbooks, written years after the events. However, we must be aware of bias in all resources. Bias is when someone is inclined to favour one view or opinion of an event over alternatives. They may choose to represent something in a particular way, or only present the reader with certain facts, to try to influence the reader's opinion one way or the other.

The 5 Ws

To assess whether or not a source is biased in some way you can use the 5 Ws: What, Who, When, Where, and Why. Asking these five questions about a source can help you determine the accuracy and relevance of the information you have in front of you. There is a difference between fact and opinion, but as we shall see throughout this chapter, both kinds of resources are valid and useful. The facts that you find, such as dates when laws were passed or organizations were formed, will form the basis of your understanding. However, the many other resources you discover, which may include more opinions than facts, will help you understand why such laws were passed or why some people fought against them.

The 5 Ws approach

What: What is the source? Is it an official document? Does it contain facts or opinions? If facts, could those facts have been chosen to present a particular view?

Who: Who wrote the letter, took the photo, or collected the statistics? What are the writer's motives for creating this message? When you know who they are, can you tell how this might have influenced their choices or writing?

When: When was the source created? How can you tell its age? If it is quite old, could it be out of date?

Where: Can you tell where it was created? If it is a piece about women in China, but was written in the UK, what might that tell you about its accuracy?

Why: Why was the source created? Does the source tell you why it was created? Can you guess why it was created?

Comparing quotes to identify bias

Look at these two quotes. One is from a woman in 1909 and the other from a male politician in 1907. Can you work out which one is which?

Quote A: *"Women's suffrage is a more dangerous leap in the dark than it was in the 1860s because of the vast growth of the Empire... and therewith the increased complexity and risk of the problems which lie before our statesmen... problems of men, only to be solved by the labour and special knowledge of men, and where the men who bear the burden ought to be left unhampered by the political inexperience of women."*

Quote B: *"Those who confuse women's character with effeminacy are strangely blind to facts... Whilst her influence in politics will be humanizing it will also be strengthening, and much of the chicanery and knavery of political life will go down before her direct march upon the actual."*

You may be surprised to know that Quote A was written by Mary Humphrey Ward (quoted in *The Times* newspaper, 27 February 1909), President of the Women's National Anti-Suffrage League who campaigned against women being given the vote. Quote B is from "The Case for Women's Suffrage" written in 1907 by James Keir Hardie, Britain's first elected Labour politician, and a supporter of women's suffrage. You can see how finding out the who, why, when, what, and where of sources helps us understand the bias better.

Artefacts are interesting primary sources, but you still need to ask who made them, when, where, and why they were made. These suffragette badges were worn by women as proud symbols of their determination to gain the vote.

Do photos ever lie?

Photos can be a true and fascinating record of past events. A photograph can sometimes bring an event alive more effectively than words alone and photographs can add interest and detail to a history report. The very existence of certain photographs can tell us interesting facts about the history of women's changing role. In 2003 the UK National Archives released photographs taken by police who were spying on suffragettes. These prove that the government regarded the suffragettes (who most people today view as heroines) as a terrorist threat. Some of the pictures show women on campaigns and others are "mug shots", pictures used for identification purposes. Some of these mug shots were, for example, circulated to art galleries and museums so they could watch out for "known militant suffragettes" after attacks on some famous works of art.

Using picture sources

While doing your research you may come across pictures that you would like to use to illustrate your research. You must however be aware of **copyright** laws. Students can usually copy and reproduce pictures from the Internet or other sources if they are used purely for their own personal research or in work that is purely for assessment. Otherwise you will need to check the terms of use for any photographs (there may be a link on the homepage of the website where you found the picture). Some sites allow free use, but others do not.

Ways of seeing

When looking at historical photographs, you need to think critically. You need to ask what is the message that the photo communicates? Does it show the suffragettes in a positive or negative light? Who took the photograph: the police, or a supporter of the suffragette cause? What was the photograph being used for: to present suffragettes as ordinary women, or as terrorists? Many photos show suffragettes chaining themselves to railings, smashing windows, or starting fires. These emphasize the threat the women posed, not the cause for which they fought. There are very few photos that show police and prison brutality against such women, some of whom were force fed using long plastic tubes when on hunger strike, or slapped and beaten. You can also use SQ3R (page 25) or the 5 Ws (page 30) to help you evaluate images.

Altered images

Photographs are rarely totally objective. Photographers can undermine the true facts of an event and this is often done on purpose. Photographers can choose to show only certain sections of a scene, or even alter prints to give a biased perspective. This can tell us as much about historic events as genuine pictures can.

These photos show a prisoner called Evelyn Manesta. The police wanted prison photos of suffragettes for their records. Some women refused to co-operate and moved to blur the pictures. Manesta was held still by a guard's arm around her neck. In a wanted poster circulated later by the police, the photo was altered. The arm around her neck was cut out and replaced by a scarf.

Letters and diaries

How useful are letters and diaries for researchers? Compared to other kinds of written sources, such as legal records, letters and diaries offer us more personal and individual views of the past. They are also interesting in terms of women's history because they are one of the few sources of information about ordinary people, in contrast to the politicians, businessmen, and other "important" people who usually get their words published. For much of history women could not achieve positions of power, so their voices were not heard, which makes reading letters and diaries by women even more significant.

Access to ordinary voices

One significant change for many women in the 20th century was the introduction of birth control. In the early 20th century, as well as deaths in childbirth itself, many women died after being weakened by giving birth to ten or more children and living in poverty. This letter from 1924 was written by the 27-year-old wife of a farm labourer to Marie Stopes (who opened the first birth-control clinics in London in 1921) asking advice on how to stop having children. It is a good example of the way letters can be a chance for researchers to hear voices that would otherwise not be heard:

> My children do not have enough to eat and I cannot buy boots for them to wear... I have got into trouble with the school, because my boy did not go, as I had no boots for him to wear... Do you think it would be best if I leave my husband and go into the workhouse... so we don't have any more children? I have gone without food and have tried to win money but everything I try fails. If you can kindly advise me I would be very grateful.

Finding these sources

The best way to see a diary extract or a letter is in its original form, for example in an archive or a museum collection. However, you are more likely to be able to access them in a book or on the Internet. Because of this it is important to find out who was involved in creating the version in front of you. Is the text you see in its original form? Did family members remove unflattering extracts before agreeing to its publication, or an editor take out bits that didn't suit the argument they wanted to present?

Examining letters and diaries

The other thing to consider when examining letters and diaries is to think about whom the writer was writing for. Letters are written to someone else, so it is easy to see how this might have influenced the writer. For example, a woman writing to a friend might be more open than she would be writing a letter to a stranger or an official. However, although diaries are written for oneself, many people wrote them knowing that they might be read in the future, and tried to present themselves in a certain way.

Diary details

This is a section from a diary written by Mabel Lincoln, a housewife in Australia, in May 1930:

> Rise 7.30 Kornies & toast, no eggs to be procured in the town, tidy up generally get to washing 11 o'clock, for dinner we have Puree made from Rice & beans I have in the meat safe & Mutton stock, boiled potatoes (in skins), tin kippered herrings, Tapioca warmed up (left from Yesterday) do three coppers full of white washing, finish at 5 PM cook scones & jam tarts for tea (pastry scraps left from yesterday makes 15 tarts) cook corn beef for tomorrow (Harold's favourite dish)...

When we first read this it sounds as if Lincoln only has two interests in life: housework and cooking! However, Australian history researcher Katie Holmes read this diary with a clear sense of its historical context. In the 1930s in Australia there was a change in the amount of advice given to women from "experts" about "domestic science" (cooking, housekeeping, and child-rearing). With this in mind, and knowing that Lincoln expected her diary might be read, we can see that she was keen to present herself as a good cook, housekeeper, wife, and mother. It tells us as much about the change in expectations of women in Australia at that time as it does about Lincoln herself.

Moving images

Here we look at how you can use moving images to research and answer questions about women in history, such as "Why did many women feel frustrated with their lives in the 1950s?", or "What can you say about the treatment of women workers after the end of World War II?" After World War II there was a major shift in the way women were treated and moving images – such as films and TV adverts – are one way of examining this change. You can watch old films by borrowing DVDs or watching when they are shown on TV. To find out which might be the most interesting or relevant, read reviews of some of the era's films in a film guidebook or on the Internet. You can also search for adverts and other film clips on websites, such as YouTube or MySpace.

Watch and learn

Many TV and cinema advertisements in the early 1950s show women in the home being happy wives and mothers. The question a researcher needs to ask in this case is what image of women were they trying to promote and why? Advertisers promoted the image of ideal women being housewives partly because governments wanted women to leave the world of work so men could have their jobs back, but for advertisers this was also an opportunity to sell products – such as the latest electrical gadgets – to make the "happy home" complete.

We can also see the influence of the changing role of women in films of the time. For example, the American film *Mildred Pierce* (1945) is about a woman who tries to succeed in business as a single parent, but ends up losing everything. What kind of message do you think this negative portrayal sent out to ambitious women in the United States and elsewhere?

Tips on evaluating moving images

When evaluating moving images remember the 5 Ws: What, Who, When, Where, and Why?
- What kind of image is it? Is it an advertisement or propaganda designed to persuade us of an opinion?
- Who made the images? Is it a company selling a lifestyle in order to sell goods or is the film company reflecting a time or mood in their stories?
- When was it made? Was it made at the time of the events it portrays?
- Where was it made? What was going on in that place at the time?
- Why was it made? What were the film-makers hoping to achieve?

*This is a **still** from "I Love Lucy", a hugely popular U.S. TV show in the 1950s and 1960s. Lucy's world is a cosy, domestic one, and images like this were thought to encourage women back into the home and away from the office. While not all women followed this role model, statistics show that there was a general shift. The average age at which women were married at this time was 20 – the youngest it had been for 60 years.*

Newspapers and magazines

Newspaper reports are fairly easy primary sources to locate. Many articles are available online or on microfiche/film at libraries and archives. You can search the archives section of specific newspaper or magazine websites (such as that of American magazine, *Time*) or you can do a more general Internet search for articles on specific themes. Many newspapers and magazines claim to give facts, but is this always the case? You need to assess the texts you read to work out whether, for example, they really are factual or whether they are argument, persuasion, or even **propaganda**.

Always consider the following points:
- Different newspapers target people with particular backgrounds and views. Some newspapers are **right-wing** or conservative, while others may be more liberal in their views. This means that while most of the facts given in them may be correct, editors may have only selected certain facts or given the facts out of context to present a particular view.
- Some newspapers select stories because they are sensational and exciting and therefore more likely to sell papers.
- Daily newspapers have to produce reports quickly. Reporters don't always have time to put their "facts" through a thorough checking procedure.

How to evaluate a newspaper report

The style of writing and choice of words (particularly of adjectives) in a report can help us understand its bias. Here are two newspaper reports printed in June 1913 after the death of Emily Davison. Davison was a militant British suffragette who died at a horse race after throwing herself in front of a horse owned by the king. These reports show the different reactions to the event in the right-wing press (*The Times*), whose readers were mainly against the suffragettes, and a **left-wing** newspaper (the *Manchester Guardian*), whose readers were likely to be more supportive. As you read, look at the underlined adjectives. Did the use of words like "reckless", "wanton", "wicked", and "unbalanced" in *The Times* article reflect or help shape public opinion at the time?

The Times

A deed of this kind, we need hardly say, is not likely to increase the popularity of any cause with the ordinary public. <u>Reckless</u> fanaticism is not regarded by them as a qualification for the franchise ... They say that the persons who <u>wantonly</u> destroy property and <u>endanger</u> innocent lives must be either desperately <u>wicked</u> or entirely <u>unbalanced</u>.

The Manchester Guardian

IMPRESSIVE LONDON PROCESSION

The procession, which was an <u>impressive</u> pageant, was watched by dense crowds ... Nearly five thousand members from all parts of the country marched in <u>undisturbed quiet and orderliness</u> behind the coffin. Perhaps what <u>impressed</u> the London mind in it all was the note of colour. Among the women who walked there were hundreds dressed in black, but at the head was a young girl in yellow silk carrying a gilt cross.

Making myths

In the 1960s and 1970s different groups of women were involved with the Women's Liberation Movement, campaigning on different issues, including equal pay, discrimination, and the over-emphasis on women's appearance. To publicize their cause one group of women demonstrated at the Miss America Pageant in 1968. They had planned to burn a selection of things, but city officials asked them not to, so instead they symbolically put some high-heeled shoes, bras, false eyelashes, and issues of women's beauty magazines in a dustbin. One newspaper ran a headline about women burning bras and the myth of bra-burning feminists was born. Why do you think the papers did this? Was it to make a more dramatic sounding story, perhaps, or to trivialize the women's arguments?

In the late 1970s, these Canadian women celebrated International Women's Day by burning a bra. Were they responding to the media myth?

Back to books

Books – both fiction and non-fiction – often reflect what is going on in a society. So the history researcher can look at how the subject matter of books changes over a period of time for evidence of shifts in society. For example, the huge change in subject matter by some women writers in the 1970s is a marker of change in women's role. Until the 1970s many of the books aimed at women were about child-rearing or how to be a good housekeeper. In the 1970s feminist and mainstream female writers flourished. Many of these books reflect the change away from the emphasis in the 1950s on women being good wives and mothers towards finding fulfillment in other ways, perhaps through careers. For example, in her book *The Feminine Mystique* (1963) Betty Friedan described her vision of the limited life of the suburban housewife as "a comfortable concentration camp", and in Germaine Greer's book *The Female Eunuch* (1970) the author likened marriage to a form of slavery.

The Feminine Mystique

Millions of women read *The Feminine Mystique* (mystique means a distinctive interest, mystery, or meaning surrounding a person or thing), and it is often credited with having started the second wave of feminism in the United States. Shown here are the opening lines from *The Feminine Mystique*. The "problem" as Friedan sees it is that many women are unfulfilled by their role as housewives. How do her words bring attention to the **stereotyping** of women and the difficulties she felt women faced in a changing world?

"The problem lay buried, unspoken for many years in the minds of American women. It was a strange stirring, a sense of dissatisfaction, a yearning that women suffered in the middle of the twentieth century in the United States. Each suburban housewife struggled with it alone. As she made the beds, shopped for groceries, matched slipcover material, ate peanut butter sandwiches with her children, chauffeured Cub Scouts and Brownies… she was afraid to ask even of herself the silent question: Is this all?"

Evaluation and variety

Remember, whatever form of resource you are using, to question it using the 5 Ws to evaluate usefulness and any bias. Research a variety of sources, from legal records to newspaper reports, and from letters to films, to get a broad understanding of the period you are studying. Sources that may include more opinions than facts still contain useful information and can give you a real sense of people's feelings and motivations. Look at diaries, films, and books within the context in which they were written to gain a deeper understanding of what they have to say.

Pseudonyms

Pseudonyms are pen or false names that authors sometimes use if they don't want to reveal their true identity. In the 19th century many women writers wrote under male names in order to get published or for their words to be taken seriously, especially as women were expected to write only about romantic or domestic subjects. For example, the famous Victorian novelist George Eliot's real name was Mary Ann Evans. Some female authors still write under pseudonyms today. Joanne Rowling, author of the Harry Potter books, was asked by Bloomsbury, her publisher, to use two initials, JK, instead of her first name because they feared that boys might be reluctant to read books written by a female author.

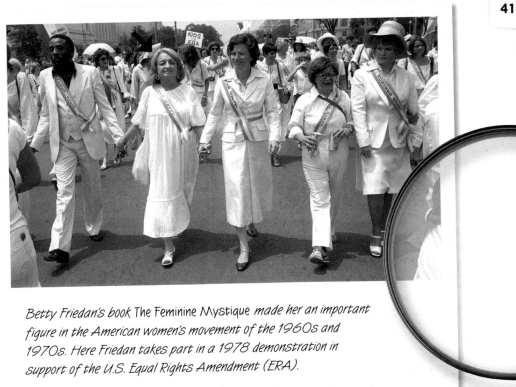

Betty Friedan's book The Feminine Mystique *made her an important figure in the American women's movement of the 1960s and 1970s. Here Friedan takes part in a 1978 demonstration in support of the U.S. Equal Rights Amendment (ERA).*

Using Your Research

Research can be fascinating and it is tempting to keep going as you discover more and more interesting facts, information, and opinions about a topic. At some point, however, you need to stop doing the research and start using it to answer your question or write your report. Now it is time to organize your research notes, sort out what you need and what you can use, and put it all together in a clear, meaningful way. Is that easier said than done?

Organizing the notes

First, clear some time and space to organize your notes. This stage is vital because it will help you to avoid repeating or missing bits of information. It will make life a lot easier for you when you come to planning and writing your piece, so try to do it when there are no distractions around. You can organize your notes in a number of different ways. You can organize notes chronologically, for example. This is according to the date when things happened. Or you could organize the information within topics, such as "women in politics","women at work", and "women's education".

Tips on sorting your notes

If you already have a rough idea of how your argument might progress in your essay or report, you could start to group your notes within sections that reflect those ideas. For example:

Ideas	Notes
1. Why the suffragettes fought for the right to vote.	
2. What tactics they used.	
3. Who opposed this change and why?	
4. When and why suffrage for women was won.	

Keeping balance

As you gather your research notes together you may find you have some pieces of conflicting information. So long as you represent both sides of the argument it is perfectly acceptable to quote different viewpoints in your report as this gives balance to your writing and a richer view of the past. For example, when discussing the suffragette issue be clear that you understand that some men supported the women's movement and some women were against the women's movement. Even female activists did not necessarily want to help *all* women – many early suffragists were fighting for the right to vote for middle- and upper-class women only, not working-class women. Keeping a balance like this avoids over-simplification of issues and proves that you have carried out wide-ranging research.

Organizing information in sections that are clearly headed and logically divided makes it easier to find things. It also saves you time when you need to pull the notes together into an essay. Having a large pile of notes can be daunting and confusing, while organizing them puts you in control of your work and helps you to be clear about how to progress.

Using graphic organizers

Graphic organizers help you to organize facts and information. This in turn will help you to express your ideas more successfully when you combine the notes in your final piece. Graphic organizers, as their name suggests, organize information in a graphic, or visual, way. There have been a variety of organizers throughout this book, such as the Venn diagram on page 9 and the timeline on page 27. They can be used in different ways. For example, Venn diagrams are useful for comparing and contrasting information and timelines are useful for comparing and contrasting events in time and for putting events into their historical context.

Fishbone maps

Most graphic organizers use key words or short sentences to fit information into a hierarchy of main or focus topic, subtopics, and details. A fishbone map is useful when a research topic has multiple strands, or elements. The idea of a fishbone map is that the central bone, or line, of the fish "skeleton" is your main idea or the point you wish to prove. This central bone has other bones coming off it that each contains a major argument about the main idea. These first ribs of the map can then have other lines coming off them to further expand a point or idea.

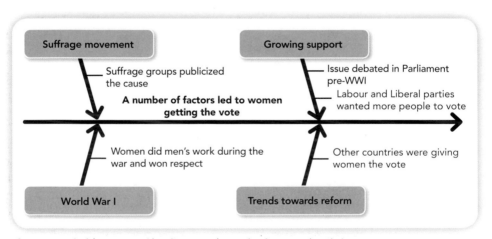

Creating a fishbone map, like this one about the factors that led to women getting the vote, helps you to organize information and be clear about the main issues.

Concept webs

A concept web or map is rather like a spider's web. There is one main heading or question in the middle. Leading out from this are various other strands, which contain the main ideas that are connected to the central theme or that answer the central question. From each of these subheadings come other bubbles or boxes that contain supporting facts and details.

Organizing facts in a web like this prepares you for writing. In this case the facts will help prepare an answer to the question: Why was the women's movement so active in the late 1960s and the 1970s?

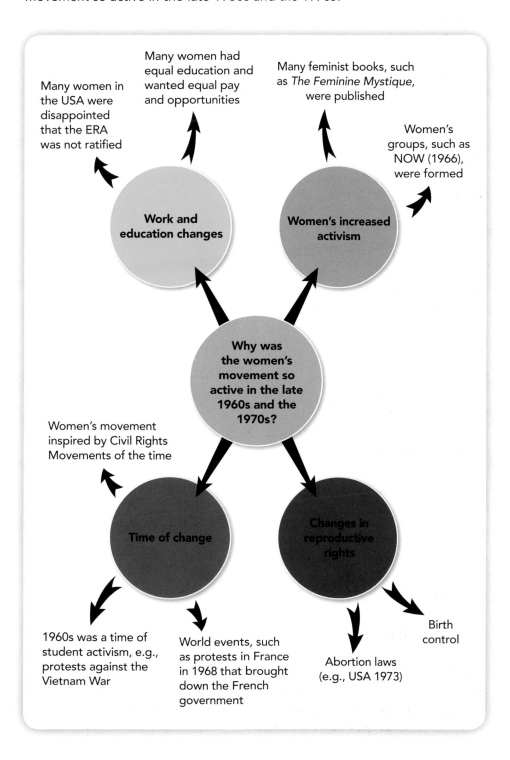

Many women in the USA were disappointed that the ERA was not ratified

Many women had equal education and wanted equal pay and opportunities

Many feminist books, such as *The Feminine Mystique*, were published

Women's groups, such as NOW (1966), were formed

Work and education changes

Women's increased activism

Why was the women's movement so active in the late 1960s and the 1970s?

Women's movement inspired by Civil Rights Movements of the time

Time of change

Changes in reproductive rights

1960s was a time of student activism, e.g., protests against the Vietnam War

World events, such as protests in France in 1968 that brought down the French government

Abortion laws (e.g., USA 1973)

Birth control

Planning your written work or presentation

Once you have sorted out your notes, and made a graphic organizer to organize your thoughts, the next step is planning how to formulate your presentation or write your report, coursework, or essay answer. For most written projects you should include at least four clear sections: an introduction, the main text containing your evidence and information, a conclusion, and endmatter, such as a list of sources.

Introduction

The introduction can take various forms. Many students use it to outline what their argument will be and how they will explain it. Just because this is first in your plan, doesn't mean you have to write it first. Some people prefer to write the introduction after they have completed the rest.

Main section

The main section of the essay usually consists of a number of paragraphs, or subheadings, within which you will develop your argument. Ideally you will plan what will go in each section before you put pen to paper. That way you can check that you have sufficient evidence and examples to demonstrate your points. At this point you can also decide where you need to present alternative points of view.

Conclusion

In the conclusion, you should recap on the key points of your answer and sum up your final argument. The endmatter is more straightforward, but there are conventions you usually have to follow when presenting book lists or giving references for quotes (see p.50).

Tips for biographies

Your work may take a different form for different kinds of reports and presentations. For example, if you are working on a biography you need to address the following questions:

- Who is the person you are writing about (age, background, etc.)?
- What events changed this person?
- What made this person famous or important?
- Why did this person in particular achieve what he or she did?
- How was this person important to other people?

What are the key differences between women's role in 1900 and today?

I. Women's role in the home has changed since 1900.
  A.   The size of families has changed.
       1. In 1900 women had large families.
       2. Today most families in West have no more than two children due to birth control (laws and dates).
  B.   Women's position at home has changed.
       1. In 1900 most middle-class women lived at home until they were married.
       2. Many women today live independently.
  C.   Women's homework
       1. In 1900 women ran the household.
       2. Today working men and women share more of the household duties, but in reality women still do the major share.

II. Women's options for occupations have changed.
  A.   In 1900 women had a limited choice of jobs.
       1. Most women in 1900 who worked did so as servants or in manual labour for low pay.
       2. Women mostly did not do same jobs as men because general belief was they were less capable and less intelligent.
  B.   In theory women can enter any occupation today.
       1. There are few women in the top jobs in their chosen profession.
       2. There is still resistance to females working in some traditionally male jobs.
       3. Although women have the right to equal pay, their pay is still often lower than men's.

III. Women's rights have changed.
  A.   Women's rights to education have changed.
       1. In 1900 few women had the right to further education.
       2. Women in West have equal right to further education.
  B.   Women's rights in law have changed.
       1. In 1900 few women had right to vote and had few legal rights.
       2. Today women have right to vote and there are laws giving them equality.

One way to plan the paragraphs you wish to include in the main body of your text, or in your oral report or presentation, is to use a graphic outline like this. This breaks a topic down into main ideas with subheadings that contain sentences about supporting facts or details. The sections are prompts for the organization of your work. Don't forget to back up the statements with facts, examples, and quotations.

Write it up!

When you are finally ready to write up your written project or essay, you should be able to follow your plan and your work will automatically have a sensible structure. That leaves you free to make it fluent and interesting, with lots of examples from your research. Try to make your text factual and explanatory. Back up clear statements and arguments with evidence and examples.

You can and should use examples of other people's persuasive texts, such as opinions in letters or quotes from adverts, but you need to try to give a balanced argument. To communicate your ideas successfully, try to write clearly. Divide the work into paragraphs and try not to make your sentences overlong or too complex.

How to use quotes

You can use quotations to illustrate a point, add credibility or support to your argument, and to show that your ideas are based on careful research. You can integrate short quotes into your main text in inverted commas. For example: "Women in World War II learned to do men's work, as Annice Gibbs, who worked for the WLA Timber Corps, remarked: '*After our training, we soon got used to heavy work, such as lifting pit-props and cutting them into various lengths for the coal mines.*'"

Start longer quotes on a new line (perhaps in italics) and include the author's surname, the year when the book or article was published, and the page on which you found it in the text, as a footnote, or in an endnote list.

The perils of plagiarism

Any report, answer or essay with your name on it is yours and you should write it in your own words, using your own research and understanding. **Plagiarism** is when someone copies another person's material and passes it off as their own and does not credit the original author. Copying from someone else's assignment or handing in an essay you downloaded from the Internet is plagiarism.

Some schools and colleges exclude students for plagiarism. This is another reason to keep a record of your research sources and quote them properly.

Using illustrations

Another way to add interest and variety to your work is to include illustrations. However, any pictures you use should add something to your argument and should not be purely decorative!

Carefully chosen pictures extend the information in the text. Include new information in picture captions rather than just repeat stuff you have already covered in the main text. (See copyright issues involved with using pictures on page 32).

Here is an example of how a picture can be used to reinforce and extend information in a text. This picture and the caption with it are intended to accompany text in a written report about the way that women increased their share of the workforce in most countries of the world during the 1970s and 1980s.

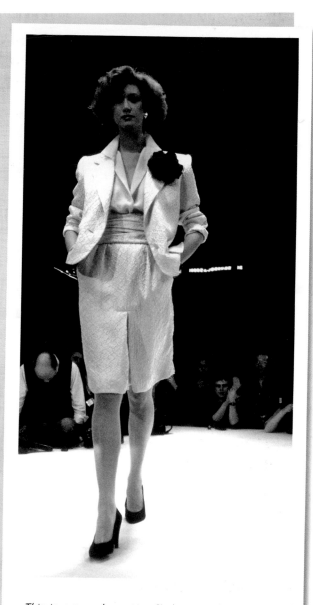

This is a sample caption: "In history, women's clothes often mirrored their function in the world. For example, in 1900 women still wore long confining dresses that echoed the fact that their lives were often confined to their homes. In the 1980s many women were increasing their power in the workplace and feminized versions of male business suits with wide shoulder pads became very popular."

Always check and edit!

Leaving work till the last minute is not only stressful, it may mean you don't get a chance to check and edit it. This would be a mistake because checking and editing is a vitally important stage in the process. Before handing in any major piece of work, try to give yourself a day or two to re-read and correct it. It might also help to ask a friend or someone in your family to go over it, too, to see if there are any places where it doesn't make sense or where a point isn't fully explained. This is also your chance to reduce the text if it is overlong, or add a paragraph if it is coming in below the expected word count. As you read through your work, make sure that it is organized into clear paragraphs or sections that are clearly related to each other.

Endmatter

The "endmatter" in a written piece of work should consist of a list of references cited and a bibliography. The bibliography is a list of details about the books, magazines, websites, and other resources you used in your research, while the list of endnotes cites those you have quoted in your report. In both cases you need to give information on the title, the author, the publisher, and the date of publication. In endnotes or footnotes you should also give the page number where the material you cited occurs. When quoting sources from the Internet, give the reader enough information to be able to locate the site easily. For example, give the author's name and the full website address. Find out from your teacher the exact format required for bibliography and endnote citations.

Presentation matters

The way you present your work matters. A well-presented piece of work is clearer and easier to read and understand and therefore more likely to be understood and marked well. Here are some tips for good presentation. If you feel you need further help, don't hesitate to ask your tutor.

Written presentation tips

- Take time to sort and organize your notes using graphic organizers.
- Plan your assignment carefully, perhaps using a graphic outline.
- Use clear, descriptive headings.
- Structure the main part of your assignment using paragraphs and developing an argument thoughtfully.
- Write in your own words with your own balanced arguments.
- Choose quotes that support your argument.
- Include a bibliography of your research sources.
- Check, edit, and refine your work before handing it in.

- Check for spelling errors.
- Read it out loud to check that the sentences are clear, and that there aren't any missing words.
- Check your punctuation. Errors in punctuation can change the sense and meaning of a phrase or sentence.
- Make sure your references (footnotes or endnotes) and bibliography are consistent and complete.

The last word

After your assignment has been handed in, and you're sitting back and contemplating the great mark you are likely to get after all your hard work, there is no need to stop doing research. People research to fulfill a brief for a particular essay or report, but they also research out of personal interest and a desire to be better informed. If the topic you've been working on really has gripped your imagination you may find that you want to go on reading and learning about it for a long time afterwards.

While some people in the West think of Muslim women as oppressed, women under the laws of the Qur'an have long had some rights that were only granted to western women in the 19th and 20th centuries, such as the right to education and to own property. Researching information like this can help create balance in reports and presentations.

Glossary

abortion termination of a pregnancy

artefact human-made object that gives us clues about how people lived in the past

biased influenced or prejudiced against someone or something

bibliography list of books or other texts usually giving the title, the author's name, the publisher, and the date of publication

birth control method used to prevent pregnancy, such as taking the contraceptive pill

chronological arrangement of events in time order, from earliest to most recent

cite to give credit to a work or author

contraception measures taken to prevent pregnancy

copyright legal right granted to an author or other person, for the exclusive publication or reproduction of their work

graphic organizer visual representation of knowledge, concepts, or ideas

illiterate unable to read or write

index alphabetical listing of names and topics that appear inside a book along with page numbers where they appear

left-wing in politics, usually associated with people or policies that place the needs of the community above the short-term wants of the individual

maternity leave mother's paid or unpaid time off work to care for a new baby

oppressed when a person or group of people are governed or treated cruelly or unjustly

paraphrase your own version of information that you have read, rewritten in your own words

plagiarism when someone copies and presents someone else's writing as their own work

primary source manuscripts, records, or documents that provide original or "first-hand" research or documentation

propaganda promotion of ideas, often using a selective version of the truth

quote/quotation copy of words of text originally published elsewhere. Direct quotations usually appear in quotation marks.

right legal or moral entitlement

right-wing in politics, usually associated with people or policies that favour individual interests over the community, and tradition over change

scanning reading technique used to find specific information quickly. You glance across a page looking out for specific words, particularly bold words, subheads, and images that appear in the text near where you find the scanned words.

secondary source research materials or sources that contain information that has been quoted, translated, or based upon another primary or original source

skimming reading technique to find out what a source contains. You read titles, introductions or first paragraphs, first sentences of every other paragraph, pictures, and summaries or last paragraphs.

SQ3R stands for Survey, Question, Read, Recite, Review. This technique guides you through finding the relevance of evidence and also remembering it through reading and reciting.

stereotype over-simplified image or representation

still single film frame from a film or TV programme used like a photograph

suffrage right to vote

suffragette woman who campaigned for the right of women to vote. Suffragettes were more militant (hands-on and forceful) than suffragists and were willing to break the law to make their views heard.

suffragist person who campaigned for the right of women to vote

summary sentence or paragraph that sums up a selection of information

UN United Nations, an international organization of independent states formed in 1945 to promote peace and security

western world political name for rich, industrialized, mainly democratically governed countries, such as those of Europe and North America

Find Out More

Books

Downing, David. *Leading Lives: Emmeline Pankhurst*. Oxford: Heinemann Library, 2002.

Hoyt-Goldsmith, Diane. *Forty Famous Women*. London: Longman, 2004.

MacDonald, Fiona. *Women in History: Peace and War, 1900–1945*. London: Chrysalis Books, 2003.

Price, Sean. *Front-Page Lives: Benazir Bhutto*. Oxford: Heinemann Library, 2010.

Ross, Mandy. *20th Century Perspectives: The Changing Role of Women*. Oxford: Heinemann Library, 2002.

Websites

At www.pbs.org/stantonanthony there is an interesting article called "Not For Ourselves Alone", which tells the stories of Americans Elizabeth Cady Stanton and Susan B. Anthony and tracks key events in the suffrage movement, shows historic documents and essays, and takes a look at where women are today.

At www.bbc.co.uk/radio4/womanshour/timeline/1900.shtml there is a women's history timeline and audio slideshow, divided into decades.

The U.S. National Organization of Women has its own website: www.now.org on which you can read pages about its history.

The UK Parliament website has information and primary source material about suffragettes at www.parliament.uk/parliamentary_publications_and_archives/parliamentary_archives/archives_the_suffragettes.cfm

There is a section on "Women, Work, and War" at www.learningcurve.gov.uk/britain1906to1918/g4/cs4/g4cs4s2.htm that covers the period 1906–1918 and it has copies of primary sources.

The Imperial War Museum has photos and posters linked to women and war and the effects of war on women's lives at "No Job for a Woman": www.iwm.org.uk/upload/package/30/women/index.htm

The UN website "WomenWatch" at www.un.org/womenwatch has information and resources on gender equality and female empowerment.

Places to visit

The International Museum of Women in San Francisco, USA, combines exhibits that celebrate and chronicle the history of women's roles in society and history: www.imow.org

The Women's Library houses the biggest collection in the UK related to women's history. Access is free and open to everyone. For opening times and special exhibition details see www.londonmet.ac.uk/thewomenslibrary

Artefacts

At www.nwhm.org/exhibits/gallery_1.html (National Women's History Museum) there is an image gallery on which you can view items such as suffrage ribbons and medals and other artefacts to do with women's changing role. There are also pages of text, pictures, and posters about the struggle for women's suffrage.

Ideas for topics to research

Here are some ideas for topics to research on the theme of the changing role of women:

- One interesting line of research would be the links between the civil rights movements and the women's rights movement, and the women involved.
- Find out more about individuals who played a major part in women's changing role in the 20th century, such as the Pankhurst family, Germaine Greer, Gloria Steinem, Betty Friedan, and others.
- Explore women's suffrage around the world, in India, China, and Japan for example, or in Egypt, researching the Egyptian Feminist Union, founded in 1923.
- Look at women in politics, such as Eleanor Roosevelt, Indira Gandhi, Benazir Bhutto, and Aung San Suu Kyi (elected leader of Burma in 1990, but not allowed to govern).
- Research the state of women's education throughout the 20th century, including the times when girls in different countries were granted the same education rights as boys.
- Research the rights and status of women in terms of marriage and divorce in different countries throughout the 20th century.
- What roles have women played in the world of the media and the arts, and how has this role changed throughout the 20th century?

Index

abortion **15, 45**
advertisements **36**
armed forces **12, 13, 16**
artefacts **7, 31**

balanced arguments **43, 48**
bias **6, 30, 31, 33, 38**
bibliographies **21, 50**
biographies **7, 46**
birth control **12, 15, 34, 45**
brainstorming **18**

copyright **32, 49**

data capture sheets **28–29**
documents **6**
  biographies **7, 46**
  letters and diaries **34–35**
  newspapers and magazines **6, 7, 37–39**

education **8, 11, 12, 14, 45**
employment **8, 9, 10–11, 12–13, 15, 48**
encyclopedias **7, 8, 21, 22**
equal rights, struggle for **9, 13, 16, 28, 29, 39, 45**

The Feminine Mystique **13, 40, 41**
films and television **7, 36–37**
first-hand accounts **5**

graphic organizers **44–45**
  concept webs **44–45**
  data capture sheets **28–29**
  fishbone maps **44**
  KWL charts **18–19**
  timelines **17, 26–27, 44**

Venn diagrams **9, 44**

healthcare **8, 15**

images **6, 49**
  altered images **33**
  copyright **32, 49**
  evaluation **32, 36**
  moving images **36–37**
  photographs **7, 32–33**
indexes **21**
Internet **6, 21, 22–23, 32, 48, 50**
  search engines **22**
  websites, useful **23**
letters and diaries **6, 7, 34–35**
libraries and archives **20, 23, 37**

marriage and divorce **8, 9, 11, 13, 37**

newspapers and magazines **6, 7, 37–39**
note-taking **6, 28**

organizing **42–43**
overview **6, 8–17**

paraphrases **28**
photographs **7, 32–33**
plagiarism **48**
politics, women in **11, 13–14, 15**
presentation **46–51**
  balanced arguments **43, 48, 51**
  checking and editing **50–51**
  endmatter **50**
  illustrations **49**
  writing plan **46, 47, 48, 50**

private and public spheres **9**

propaganda **37**
pseudonyms **41**

quotations **28, 31, 48**

reference books **6, 7, 8, 20–21**
research
  organizing **6, 42–45**
  skimming and scanning **24**
  SQ3R technique **25, 32**
research process **6, 29**

sources
  5 Ws test **30, 32, 36, 40**
  citation **28, 50**
  cross-checking **6, 26**
  primary **6, 7**
  quality and accuracy **22, 26, 30, 37, 38, 40–41**
  secondary **6, 7**
sport **12, 27**
suffrage (voting rights) **4, 5, 8, 9, 10, 11, 14, 31, 43**
suffragettes and suffragists **10, 19, 31, 32, 33, 38, 43**

timelines **17, 26–27, 44**
topic narrowing and broadening **19**
tradition and religious beliefs **16, 51**

women's movement **9, 13, 39, 40, 41, 45**
women's role and status
  overview **8–17**
  timeline **17**
World Wars **5, 10–11, 12, 36**